YEAR 7 ENGLISH
TECHNIQUES

- Transfer Framework skills to test

- Reading, writing and spelling preparation

- Tackle question styles and types

- Review and revise text types

Keith Brindle

Acknowledgements

United Kingdom: Folens Publishers, Apex Business Centre, Boscombe Road, Dunstable, LU5 4RL.
Email: folens@folens.com

Ireland: Folens Publishers, Greenhills Road, Tallaght, Dublin 24.
Email: info@folens.ie

Poland: JUKA, ul. Renesansowa 38, Warsaw 01-905

Editor: Caroline Kellord
Layout artist: Suzanne Ward
Illustrations: Margaret Jones
Cover design: Ed Gallagher
Cover image: PhotoDisc/Getty Images

Text:
page 10 'You can't catch me' by Juliette Maxam/*The Sunday Express* 24 June 2001.
page 12 *A Cellarful of Noise – Beatlemania*, by Brian Epstein, published by Souvenir Press Ltd © 1964.
page 21 From *Groosham Grange*/ Text copyright © 1988 Anthony Horowitz. Published by Egmont Books Limited and used with permission.
page 41 'The Fun They Had' from *Earth is Room Enough* by Isaac Asimov, published by Doubleday Broadway Publishing Group, 1969.

Extracts are presented in their original form; therefore some spellings may not be in common use today.

Images:
page 10 John Searle/ACE Photo Agency.
page 14 Reproduced by permission of the DfES.
page 37 Jean Heguy/CORBIS.

First published 2002 by Folens Limited.

British Library Cataloguing in Publication Data. A catalogue record for this publication is available from the British Library.

ISBN 1-84303-010-1

Contents

Checklist of the key areas you will cover in this book, and the main objectives from the Framework for English for Year 7.

Unit	Focus	Selected Objectives
1	*Knowing the papers; awareness of text types*	Sentence level 13
2	*Examining different types of text; how texts operate at word, sentence and whole text level*	Paragraphing and cohesion 9 Research and study skills 4 Understanding the author's craft 12, 13 Reading for meaning 7, 8, 9, 10
3	*Types of question and how to interpret them; conveying information in different ways*	Research and study skills 1, 2 Reading for meaning 7, 8
4	*What is being assessed in the test; the different types of reading skill required and how to respond in writing*	Research and study skills 1, 2, 5 Reading for meaning 7, 8, 11 Inform, explain, describe 11 Understanding the author's craft 13
5	*Focusing on priorities in the test; organising time and answers*	Research and study skills 5 Inform, explain, describe 11
6	*Employ a structured writing process; plan and draft work effectively*	Plan, draft, present 1, 2, 3 Spelling strategies 8, 12
7	*Revising writing to persuade, argue, advise*	Persuade, argue, advise 15, 16, 17 Paragraphing and cohesion 12
8	*Revising writing to inform, explain, describe*	Inform, explain, describe 10, 11, 12, 13, 14
9	*Getting to know the demands of the spelling test; revising key conventions of spelling*	Spelling 1–7
10	*Revising key elements of the test, and the skills involved*	Research and study skills 1, 2

Using this book

Q **Why do I need this book?**

A Although you should have covered the range of skills assessed by the tests, it is not always easy to transfer what you know into a test situation.

Q **But if I already know how to write informatively, or read carefully, I should be OK, shouldn't I?**

A Tests are rather different from the day-to-day English work you do in class. For a start, you have stricter time limits, and you are working very much on your own. These things are not always easy to cope with.

Q **So, how will this book help?**

A It will make very clear what is required in the tests you will take, and draw attention to some key areas you may have covered in English, but may need to revisit. It will also help you understand what different questions expect from you, and how to show what you know, rather than what you don't.

Q **Why is the book divided into Units?**

A Each Unit deals with a different aspect of the tests. For example, in the first half of the book the focus is on the Reading test. Unit 3 ('Types of question') explains the difference between simple 'information only' questions and how to recognise them, and 'explanation and quotation' questions. Later Units deal with the Writing test, reminding you of key differences between writing to persuade and advise, for example.

Q **Is there anything else to improve my chances of test success?**

A Each Unit tells you clearly at the start what you will be focusing on. There are also regular '**Examiner's Tips**' provided by the author which provide useful hints on aspects of the test. The '**Further Work**' sections give you a chance to do that little bit extra, if you feel the need. In addition, you will see that each Unit ends with a '**Summary**'. If nothing else, you can use that as a mini 'revision card' to keep ideas in your head.

The page opposite shows these features.

Q **Before I start, how should I use the book … in school, or at home?**

A The book is designed for your teacher to use in a series of lessons running up to the tests, or for you to dip into as and when you feel the need. There are a small number of tasks you can do with a friend, but the book is really aimed for your independent use. Whichever way you use it, it should help you feel prepared, and give you the best chance of test success.

Good luck!

Key features to help you

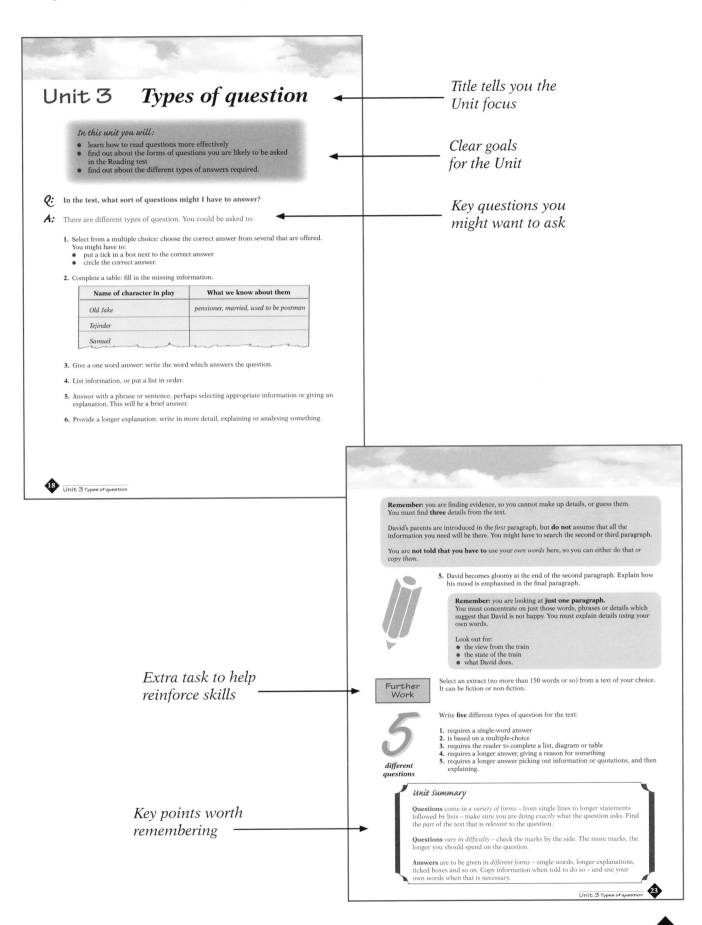

Unit 3 Types of question

In this unit you will:
- learn how to read questions more effectively
- find out about the forms of questions you are likely to be asked in the Reading test
- find out about the different types of answers required.

Q: In the test, what sort of questions might I have to answer?

A: There are different types of question. You could be asked to:

1. Select from a multiple choice: choose the correct answer from several that are offered. You might have to:
   - put a tick in a box next to the correct answer
   - circle the correct answer.

2. Complete a table: fill in the missing information.

Name of character in play	What we know about them
Old Jake	*pensioner, married, used to be postman*
Tejinder	
Samuel	

3. Give a one word answer: write the word which answers the question.

4. List information, or put a list in order.

5. Answer with a phrase or sentence, perhaps selecting appropriate information or giving an explanation. This will be a brief answer.

6. Provide a longer explanation: write in more detail, explaining or analysing something.

Title tells you the Unit focus

Clear goals for the Unit

Key questions you might want to ask

Remember: you are finding evidence, so you cannot make up details, or guess them. You must find **three** details from the text.

David's parents are introduced in the *first* paragraph, but **do not** assume that all the information you need will be there. You might have to search the second or third paragraph.

You are **not told that you have to** use your *own* words here, so you can either do that *or* copy them.

5. David becomes gloomy at the end of the second paragraph. Explain how his mood is emphasised in the final paragraph.

Remember: you are looking at **just one paragraph.** You must concentrate on just those words, phrases or details which suggest that David is not happy. You must explain details using your own words.

Look out for:
- the view from the train
- the state of the train
- what David does.

Further Work

Select an extract (no more than 150 words or so) from a text of your choice. It can be fiction or non-fiction.

5 *different questions*

Write **five** different types of question for the text:

1. requires a single-word answer
2. is based on a multiple-choice
3. requires the reader to complete a list, diagram or table
4. requires a longer answer, giving a reason for something
5. requires a longer answer picking out information or quotations, and then explaining.

Unit Summary

Questions come in *a variety of forms* – from single lines to longer statements followed by lists – make sure you are doing *exactly* what the question asks. Find the *part* of the text that is *relevant* to the question.

Questions *vary in difficulty* – check the marks by the side. The more marks, the longer you should spend on the question.

Answers are to be given in *different forms* – single words, longer explanations, ticked boxes and so on. Copy information when told to do so – and use your own words when that is necessary.

Extra task to help reinforce skills

Key points worth remembering

Unit 1   *The test explained*

In this unit you will learn about:
- what the test involves
- what, exactly, you are required to do.

There are actually three tests:

1. Reading
2. Writing
3. Spelling – which you may or may not be expected to do: your teacher will tell you whether you are one of the lucky ones!

The Reading and Writing tests both last for 75 minutes (plus 15 minutes reading time). In other ways, they are quite different.

The Reading Test

You will be given a Reading booklet which contains texts.
There are likely to be three texts, and the forms of writing covered will be:

- literary – writing that contains more than just facts: possibly imaginative writing or writing that involves feelings, uses strong images, and so on
- non-literary – concerned with giving information, and often quite formal.

These forms will be either:

- fiction – writing based on imagined situations with characters and stories

or
- non-fiction – writing referring to real events, and mainly factual information.

novel
poem
magazine article
advertisement
instructions
information leaflet
travelogue

personal letter
biography
poster
playscript
brochure
school textbook

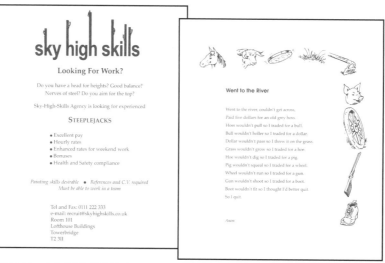

Examiner's Tip:
Take care! Non-fiction writing can often share features with fiction. For example, travel writing may be about a real journey, but include very personal feelings, strong images and powerful language.

Task 1

1. Take three of the genres on page 6. List the key features they would have; for example:

   - layout/look
   - type of language
   - use of illustration.

2. Note down any other genres that are not on the list.

The Length of the Reading Test

You will be given:
- 15 minutes to read through the test paper
- 75 minutes to answer the questions.

You will be expected to answer all the questions – there are likely to be about 20. There will be:
- questions on each of the texts
- a final question which links all the texts together.

Brighton, on the south coast of England, is a popular spot for day-trippers, and is only one hour by train from London. The following article is taken from the 'Travel' section of a Sunday newspaper.

Sea Change

When I told the children that 'summer holiday' this year meant 'Brighton', they looked at me with a mixture of shock and betrayal. "Brighton?" my eldest said, as if trying to get his head around the notion. "You mean, like, England?" said the youngest, as if I'd just told her the Titanic had appeared in our back garden. "But there's nothing to do in England," added the middle one, scornfully.

"Yes, Brighton," I confirmed, making sure there could be no mistake. I proceeded to explain that this was due to their father's finances and the need to take only a short holiday due to some time I'd used up earlier in the year. In any case, I added, "It's important you get to see your own coastline." We would not be going to Majorca, Cyprus, Crete, or any of the other places they deem 'cool'. In my case, I usually find them, in contrast, too hot. "You'll enjoy it," I said, more in hope than expectation.

Two weeks later, we found ourselves settled in a largish B&B in Kemp Town, a district to the east side of Brighton. The children looked in vain for a sparkling ice-blue swimming-pool, and frowned at the goldfish pond on the patio. The place was run by a ruddy-faced woman, Mrs Fisher, and her husband, who used to do donkey rides on the sand when the tide was out, until the donkey got too old and had to move into the local donkey retirement home (well, that's what I told the children).

"There's plenty to do here," Mrs Fisher insisted when she saw the look on the children's faces as we took up residence in our large family room. "There's the Pavilion, the Museum, the Pier – and that's just for starters. Now, who'd like a bacon sandwich, and a glass of lemonade?" The children perked up a little, and an hour later we were walking down the steep hill into the centre of town. And, as soon as they saw the Brighton Pier, the first glimmer of hope that this might not be 'The Worst Holiday Ever', appeared in their eyes.

An hour and a half later, having used up the money I'd given each of them, the three of them had to be dragged away. They'd done all the traditional stuff – trying to pick up a cheap toy with a motorised crane in a glass box, tried slot machines and pinball wizards for the first time, as well as games on modern electronic stands that were a match for Playstation and Nintendo. They had each consumed an overpriced swirly ice cream with a flake, and insisted on running to the end of the pier where they could hang perilously over the railings.

"Where are we going now, Dad?" asked the middle one, tugging me by the sleeve.

"Aren't you tired?" I asked, hopefully.

8   YEAR 7 ENGLISH QCA TEST TECHNIQUES TEACHER BOOK   © Folens Ltd (copiable page)

Sea Changes

Questions 1–9 are about *Sea Change* (pages 8–9)

1. Look at page 8.

   a) Find and copy **one** word from the first paragraph which suggests that the children are not keen to spend their holiday in Brighton.

   _____

   (1 mark)   Q1a

   b) *The children looked in vain for a sparkling ice-blue swimming-pool, and frowned at the goldfish pond on the patio.*

   Explain what this shows about the children's attitude to the place they are staying.

   _____
   _____

   (1 mark)   Q1b

2. The writer describes his youngest child's reaction to his holiday plans in the following way: *as if I'd just told her the Titanic had appeared in our back garden.*

   What is the writer trying to tell us about her reaction?

   _____
   _____
   _____

   (1 mark)   Q2

3. Here are four subheadings that **could** be used in the article. Tick the one that would be MOST suitable for paragraph 3.

   a) A trip to the pier   ☐

   b) Arrival at the B&B   ☐

   c) Hearing the news   ☐

   d) Shop till you drop   ☐

   (1 mark)   Q3

© Folens Ltd (copiable page)   YEAR 7 ENGLISH QCA TEST TECHNIQUES TEACHER BOOK   15

The Writing Test

You will have to complete two pieces of writing:

- a **major task**, which will take longest and for which you will be able to make some of the decisions about what to write
- a **minor task**, in which you will be told more precisely what to do.

In Year 7, you write to: *inform, explain, describe, persuade, argue, advise*

In Year 8, you will write to: *imagine, explore, entertain analyse, review, comment*

You will be marked on your ability to produce:

- imaginative ideas
- texts that are appropriate to topic, audience and purpose
- structured writing, in paragraphs
- varieties of sentences
- accurate punctuation
- appropriate and effective expression
- writing in which the spelling is correct.

Task 2

Consider the list above and decide which points are:
1. your strengths, on which you can build
2. the areas in which you need to improve.

The Length of the Writing Test

You will be given:
- 75 minutes to plan and write your answers.

You will not be expected to write your responses without any preparation. For each task, you will be given **a planning sheet**, to develop your ideas.

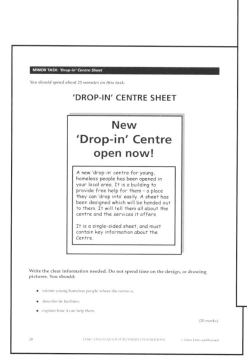

The Spelling Test

1. You will be given a text with 20 words missing.
2. Your teacher will read the text to you, including the words that have been left out of your version.
3. Your teacher will read it again, this time pausing after each word omitted from your version, so that you can write in the missing word.

English

YEAR 7

SPELLING **LEVELS 4–6**

Total marks [ ]

Name _____

Class _____

Teacher _____

Date _____

Traffic Hell

Drivers heading for Brighton for _____ Bank Holiday   *1*

were _____ in 27 miles of traffic jams in the Sussex   *2*

_____ .   *3*

_____ on the M23 motorway, the jams stretched all the   *4*

way to the outskirts of Brighton itself_____ stopped their   *5*

cars, and sat by the side of the road in the _____   *6*

temperatures. The Met Office reported that highs of 34 degrees centigrade

were recorded in early afternoon.

Not _____ , tempers frayed and there were several   *7*

_____ between drivers. However, some saw the funny   *8*

side of things, and new friends were made, as well as

_____ . Once people arrived at the coast they soon found   *9*

© Folens Ltd (copiable page)   YEAR 7 ENGLISH QCA TEST TECHNIQUES TEACHER BOOK   31

Unit Summary

◆ There are three tests: Reading, Writing and Spelling.

◆ The Reading test will take 15 minutes plus 75 minutes, involve three texts and about 20 questions.

◆ The Writing test will take 75 minutes: you will plan and write a major and minor response. You have planning sheets to help you.

◆ The Spelling test will involve 20 spellings and is not timed.

Unit 2 *Reading text types*

In this unit you will:

- examine different types of text
- see how they present ideas
- learn how to read them more effectively.

Each text will have its own style and, often, its own features of layout. In this Unit, we will look at some examples.

Newspaper reporting

You can't catch me
by Juliette Maxam

For Foster the flyaway vulture, a taste for freedom is proving to be a right carrion. Zoo staff were confident they had got their bird yesterday when the escaped predator walked into their carefully-set trap.

But with one mighty flap of his 8ft wingspan, the African Ruppell vulture broke out of the snare to soar free again.

Falconers from Banham Zoo, Norfolk, where Foster left captivity behind last Monday, spent all day in Reydon, Suffolk, yesterday trying to lure him with a succession of traps – from a noose made of string to a baited trap made of feathers stuck in the ground and tied together with string.

The bird ignored the feather trap altogether and snatched the bait from the noose without getting inside. But the team thought they had him when Foster landed on a vicarage lawn and tentatively crept forward, driven on by the scent of a chick under a camouflaged net. Slowly, slowly, head held low, he walked right into the trap. A string was pulled and for a moment Foster was caught.

But before the watching crowd could raise a single cheer, Foster stretched out his wings, shook his head, stepped clear of the net and took off to the safety of the vicarage roof.

John Dickson, head of the falconry team, said: "We are gutted and absolutely deflated. It is the best chance we have had of catching him so far – but he is so powerful he managed to pull his way out. We might have to redesign the trap and add more netting to tangle him up. He is definitely a clever bird.

"The chances are he might go in it again tomorrow. I have been saying all along that we will get him. He is not a wild bird. He is tame and each day he will get hungrier and more inclined to try to get food."

Since his escape, Foster has been trying out seaside resorts in East Anglia – travelling nearly 100 miles and favouring ecclesiastical perches. In Reydon, he tends to settle on the roof of the vicarage during the day and roost in a Scots Pine tree in the garden at night.

Super vulture finds a Foster home.

Foster has been dive bombed by sea gulls and other birds angry with him for invading their territory, but has stubbornly held his ground.

The parish priest, the Reverend Barry Naylor, who locked away his two cats when Foster appeared, said: "He seems to enjoy being in my garden. It could be because there is a long expanse of lawn which makes him feel at home."

Sunday Express, 24 June 2001

Ways of looking at the text

FOCUS Text construction

1. Layout/Presentation

You could focus on:
- the headline – and why it has been used
- the picture – the way it fits, or adds to the report
- the caption – how it fits, or adds to the picture and report
- the shape and organisation of the lines – why columns are used.

| **Task 1** | Explain to a partner why this report has used these devices. Could any other features of layout have been used here? |

2. The text as a whole

You could focus on:
- the purpose of particular paragraphs (for example, the first two, and the final one)
- how the opening is developed
- why the journalist included John Dickson's words
- new elements added to the report in the penultimate paragraph.

| **Task 2** | Look at these things, then write down how the report has been constructed and why. |

3. Particular sentences

You could focus on specific descriptions of people, events and so on, for example, what impression do we get of Foster from this sentence: *'But with one mighty flap of his 8ft wingspan, the African Ruppell vulture broke out of the snare to soar free again.'*?

The use of quotations:
'We are gutted and absolutely deflated.'
What does this add to the report?

| **Task 3** | Note down, briefly, how these sentences indicate who the readers should admire? |

4. Important words

You could focus on specific grammar forms (nouns, adverbs and so on), or choice of vocabulary (formal, informal words). For example, all these words are used in the report:
'carrion'
'noose'
'Slowly, slowly'
'gutted, deflated'.

| **Task 4** | Choose two of the above quotations, and explain what they add to the report. |

Autobiography

The Beatles were the most successful group in the history of pop: John Lennon, Paul McCartney, George Harrison and Ringo Starr changed the music business for ever. They started at the Cavern – a small club in Liverpool – and went on to conquer the world. In this extract from his autobiography, their manager, Brian Epstein, is explaining what it was like in 1963 when 'Beatlemania' was just beginning:

In Newcastle – and this was typical – nearly four thousand Beatle fans had queued in freezing conditions for tickets. Said the *Telegraph*: 'It looked more like a death watch than the prelude of a joyous Beatle event … . Three ambulances, rarely short of patients, some of them school girls, dealt with more than a hundred cases of fainting or exhaustion. Several were treated at hospital. Seventy-four police were on duty and special check points had to be set up.'

At Hull there were still three thousand in a Beatle queue after five thousand tickets had been sold. A senior police officer told the *Daily Telegraph*: 'This has been an incredible night,' and at Coventry a theatre manager said: 'I have never known anything like it. The queues and the excitement are beyond belief.'

It was the same throughout Britain. The Beatles had ceased to be purely a pop group and were becoming a cult. The concerts themselves were wild and exciting, and successful to an extent I had never thought possible. Every ticket could have been sold twice over, and after the early scenes of the ticket queues the concerts themselves consolidated the view of everyone in show business that the Beatles were the biggest thing since Sinatra in the 1940's. All of us involved with them – everyone who had known them at the Cavern – were serenely proud.

When, on October 31, the Beatles arrived home from Sweden they could not believe what they heard. Thousands of howling, screaming fans had converged on London airport hours before their plane was due in, and crush barriers had been erected to keep the youngsters from the tarmac. Paul said later: 'It has all been happening in England while we were away. We were amazed because although we had had several No. 1's in the record charts, teenage interest had only been on the normal, pop level.'

There were questions in Parliament about the queues and about the safety of teenagers outside theatres. 'Shouldn't we,' suggested one M.P., 'withdraw the police and see what happens,' and George told a reporter: 'If they do, the injuries would be their own fault. We don't want people to get hurt.'

Curiously, though mob-attention had never been more dramatic or extensive, there was no violence. I am not being priggish when I say that the Beatles have never been associated with actual rioting, vandalism or damage of any sort, I don't know why this is so, but it is.

Brian Epstein

Unit 2 Reading text types

Ways of looking at the text

1. Layout/Presentation

There is no illustration with this text, and it is written in continuous prose so the 'shape/layout' cannot be commented on directly. Does it need images? If it does, can you suggest what images might have added something to the text?

Task 5   Explain whether the text has been presented effectively.

2. The text as a whole

How does Epstein present the Beatles in this extract?

Consider:
- the excitement over tickets
- the group's feelings as they return
- the quotations
- Parliament
- the final paragraph.

Task 6   What sort of image of the Beatles is their manager hoping to create in his autobiography?

3. Particular sentences

The world was different 40 years ago, when these events took place. What in this sentence indicates it was different back then?

> *'Three ambulances, rarely short of patients, some of them school girls, dealt with more than a hundred cases of fainting or exhaustion.'*

How is the excitement made vivid in this sentence?

> *'Thousands of howling, screaming fans had converged on London airport hours before their plane was due in, and crush barriers had been erected to keep the youngsters from the tarmac.'*

4. Important words

Epstein says the Beatles were changing from 'a pop group' to a 'cult'.
Use a dictionary to find out what he means.

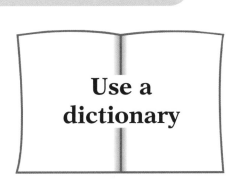

Use a dictionary

Task 7   According to Epstein, how were the Beatles changing?

Advertising

Look at this advertisement.

1. *Layout/Presentation*

Task 8

Complete this assessment of the way the advertisement is presented:

'The layout of this advertisement would probably appeal to boys/girls/boys and girls because ...'.

Task 9

Explain why these devices have been used:

● The main design of the youngsters running.	Does the advertisement look like it's advertising a love story or a science fiction thriller or ... what? Explain how and why.
● The swirling vortex through which they are running.	Does it make the situation appear confusing and/or threatening? Explain your opinion.
● The words and the number in larger fonts.	Are they designed to grab the reader's attention because of: ● the punctuation ● how they are set out ● the kinds of fonts used? Consider each bullet point in detail.
● The text box at the bottom.	Is it supposed to keep separate the more serious information? Is it effective?

2. *The text as a whole*

Task 10

How is the language used trying to attract the reader to a Modern Apprenticeship? Consider:

● the impression given by the words in larger font
● what is said beneath them, and the mood the words are trying to create.

3. *Particular sentences*

Task 11

Why is 'Make A Date With The Future!' a clever phrase to use?

4. *Important words*

Task 12

Complete this sentence:
The term 'Kick Start' at the end of the advertisement makes the reader think of ... and this is appropriate because ... .

Further Work

Choose any advertisement which features both images and text. Attach it to a larger sheet of paper and then annotate it with comments on the five areas mentioned in the Unit Summary.

Poetry

The Streets of Laredo

As I walked out in the streets of Laredo,
As I walked out in Laredo one day,
I spied a poor cowboy all wrapped in white linen,
Wrapped up in white linen, as cold as the clay.

'I see by your outfit that you are a cowboy,'
These words he did say as I boldly stepped by.
'Come sit down beside me and hear my sad story;
I was shot in the breast and I know I must die.

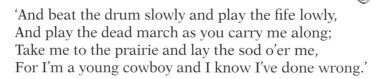

'Once in my saddle I used to look handsome,
Once in my saddle I used to look gay.
I first went to drinkin' and then to card playin',
Got shot in the breast, which ended my day.

'Let sixteen gamblers come handle my coffin,
Let sixteen girls come carry my pall;
Put bunches of roses all over my coffin,
Put roses to deaden the clods as they fall.

'And beat the drum slowly and play the fife lowly,
And play the dead march as you carry me along;
Take me to the prairie and lay the sod o'er me,
For I'm a young cowboy and I know I've done wrong.'

We beat the drum slowly and played the fife lowly,
And bitterly wept as we bore him along;
For we all loved our comrade so brave, young and handsome,
We loved the young cowboy although he'd done wrong.

Traditional

Task 13

The following is part of a response to the question:
'What is the structure of this ballad?'
Complete it.

'The poem is set out in regular stanzas and it also has regular …
This makes it sound like … a song/ a prayer/ a chant.'

Task 14

What impression of the cowboy do we get?
Write about:
- his appearance
- his past
- what he did wrong
- his funeral
- the final thoughts about him.

Task 15

'I spied a poor cowboy all wrapped in white linen,
Wrapped up in white linen, as cold as the clay.'

Read these explanations by two students about how effective the description is:

> **Stephanie:**
> *The lines are good. The cowboy has no money and is only wearing a white shirt. He is very cold.*

> **Usman:**
> *The lines give a clear picture of the cowboy's situation. We feel sorry for him, because the narrator describes him as "a poor cowboy". We think he is going to die, because of the simile "as cold as the clay". Also, the "white linen" makes us think of a shroud …*

Say which is the better answer. Give reasons.

Task 16

This is an old ballad, and some of the words are little used today, or their meanings might have changed; for example, 'gay' once meant light-hearted and carefree.

1. What, do you think, is the meaning of 'pall'?
    a. a gun
    b. a saddle
    c. a funeral cloth

Unit Summary

Understanding of a text and how it is constructed involves a number of things:
- layout and presentation
- story or message in the whole text
- overall development or structure of ideas
- effectiveness of particular sentences
- power of individual words or phrases.

Unit 3   Types of question

In this unit you will:

- learn how to read questions more effectively
- find out about the forms of questions you are likely to be asked in the Reading test
- find out about the different types of answers required.

Q: In the test, what sort of questions might I have to answer?

A: There are different types of question. You could be asked to:

1. Select from a multiple choice: choose the correct answer from several that are offered. You might have to:
    - put a tick in a box next to the correct answer
    - circle the correct answer.

2. Complete a table: fill in the missing information.

Name of character in play	What we know about them
Old Jake	pensioner, married, used to be postman
Tejinder	
Samuel	

3. Give a one word answer: write the word which answers the question.

4. List information, or put a list in order.

5. Answer with a phrase or sentence, perhaps selecting appropriate information or giving an explanation. This will be a brief answer.

6. Provide a longer explanation: write in more detail, explaining or analysing something.

Practice question

Read this poem, then answer the questions which follow:

My Husband Loved His Dog

My husband wanted a dog
and he got one.
It was shaggy and he told it his stories
and the dog laughed, in its own way.
Probably more than I did.
I had heard them all before.

Instead of taking me out for a meal,
my husband took the dog for a walk.
Often the walks were long
and involved a tour of local pubs
where the locals took to the dog
much more than they ever took to me.

But I had my place in the scheme of things
and bought the tinned food
and the flea powder
and the biscuits to keep its teeth sharp
and a new collar when it was needed
and the bones from the butcher.

When the BSE fears were at their height
I told my husband there was nothing to fear
and that infected cattle would not harm humans;
and I went on cooking beef every day
for my husband and for his dog.
Even though I had become vegetarian.

Sylvie Hawkins

Questions

1. Complete the following sentence, by selecting one word from those below:

   'The man who owned the dog sounds ...'

   a. old **b.** loving **c.** selfish

2. Fill in the missing information:

The husband treated the dog to	
For the dog, the wife provided	

3. Which lines suggest that the woman might have been a disappointment to her husband?

4. What is suggested by the title: 'My Husband Loved His Dog'?

Levels of difficulty

Q: Are some questions harder than others?

A: Some questions require more detailed reference to the text.
You could be asked to:

1. *Find and copy* a word or piece of information.

2. *Put information into order*: which will mean reading through part or all of the text.

3. *Explain*, giving reasons: you need to prove what you say by referring to the text.

4. *Find evidence*: you will have to find words or phrases in the text.

5. *Answer a complicated question*, which has a main stem that is followed by bullet points. You have to keep the stem of the question in mind, whilst writing about each bullet point in turn.

For example:

In Sylvie Hawkins' poem, what do we learn about the wife and the life she leads? In your answer, write about:
- **the sort of husband she has and what she thinks of him**
- **her role in the relationship**
- **her attitude to him and the dog in the final stanza.**

You can view questions as having three levels of difficulty:

Low level: *Find/quote information:* the easiest … no need to explain why you have chosen it, or what it means.

Mid level: *Explain only:* perhaps more difficult, but no need to find the information … that's been done already!

Top level: *Find, quote and explain:* the most difficult, but gives you the chance to put more of 'yourself' into the answer.

Task 2

Complete this answer to the complicated question above:

The wife only gives a few details about her life. However, her husband seems to get his own way …

In the relationship, it appears she is reduced to being left at home and doing the shopping for the dog …

When we first read the final stanza, we might think that the wife is very caring towards both her husband and the dog. When she mentions BSE, though, and the fact that she has become a vegetarian …

Q: **What, exactly, will the questions concentrate on?**

A: You will have to answer questions about:

1. *individual words*

2. *particular sentences*

3. *particular parts of the text*: possibly a paragraph or a text box or illustration

4. *the whole text*: you might have to decide, for example, how an argument is developed or the atmosphere is built or how a character is presented.

Task 3

Read the text below, then work through the exemplar questions.

David is setting off to his new boarding school:

David arrived at Liverpool Street Station at twelve o'clock. True to his word, his father had sent him on the bus. His mother hadn't come either. She had gone into hysterics on the doorstep and Mr Eliot had been forced to break a milk bottle over her head to calm her down. So David was quite alone as he dragged his suitcase across the forecourt and joined the queue to pick up his ticket.

It was a long queue – longer, in fact, than the trains everyone was waiting to get on. David had to wait more than twenty minutes before he reached a window and it was almost one o'clock before he was able to run for his train. A seat had been reserved for him – the school had arranged that – and he just had time to heave his case on to the luggage rack and sit down before the whistle went and the train began to move. Pressing his face against the glass, he stared out. Slowly the train picked up speed and London shuddered and rattled away. It had begun to rain. The scene could hardly have been more gloomy if he had been sitting in a hearse on the way to his own funeral.

Half an hour later they had travelled through the suburbs and the train was speeding past a number of dreary fields – all fields look much the same when they're seen through a train window, especially when the window is covered with half an inch of dust. David hadn't time to buy himself a book or comic, and anyway his parents hadn't given him any money. Dejectedly, he slumped back into his seat and prepared to sit out the three hour journey to King's Lynn.

From *Groosham Grange* by Anthony Horowitz

Questions

1. In the first paragraph, it says: *'She had gone into hysterics on the doorstep and Mr Eliot had been forced to break a milk bottle over her head to calm her down.'*
   Do you think the novel is likely to be:
   a. a horror story
   b. a mystery story
   c. humorous
   d. a fable?
   Write down one of these options as your answer.

   > **Remember:** choose just one answer from the list.
   > Read the sentence carefully and do not simply guess when making your choice.

2. *Find* a *word* which suggests that David had trouble moving his case, and *copy* it.

   > **Remember:** you are looking for just one word, and you are not being asked to explain it.
   > A suitable word in the second paragraph is 'heave'. Can you find one in the first paragraph?

3. Put the following details into chronological order – the order in which they happened. Copy out the sentences, then put a number into the box beside each statement.

   The first one has been done for you.

   David became miserable   ☐

   David arrived at Liverpool Street Station   ☐

   David stood in a queue   ☐

   David went for the bus on his own   1

   > **Remember:** you are likely to have to read right through the text to answer this sort of question.
   > Stay alert! Notice that the first sentence in this extract does **not** describe the first thing that happened. You must pay attention to exactly what is happening in the text.

4. Find **three** pieces of evidence which suggest that David's parents are not fond of him.

3

pieces of evidence

Remember: you are finding evidence, so you cannot make up details, or guess them. You must find **three** details from the text.

David's parents are introduced in the *first* paragraph, but **do not** assume that all the information you need will be there. You might have to search the second or third paragraph.

You are **not told that you have to** use your *own words* here, so you can either do that *or copy them.*

5. David becomes gloomy at the end of the second paragraph. Explain how his mood is emphasised in the final paragraph.

> **Remember:** you are looking at **just one paragraph.**
> You must concentrate on just those words, phrases or details which suggest that David is not happy. You must explain details using your own words.
>
> Look out for:
> - the view from the train
> - the state of the train
> - what David does.

Further Work

Select an extract (no more than 150 words or so) from a text of your choice. It can be fiction or non-fiction.

different questions

Write **five** different types of question for the text:

1. requires a single-word answer
2. is based on a multiple-choice
3. requires the reader to complete a list, diagram or table
4. requires a longer answer, giving a reason for something
5. requires a longer answer picking out information or quotations, and then explaining.

Unit Summary

Questions come in *a variety of forms* – from single lines to longer statements followed by lists – make sure you are doing *exactly* what the question asks. Find the *part* of the text that is *relevant* to the question.

Questions *vary in difficulty* – check the marks by the side. The more marks, the longer you should spend on the question.

Answers are to be given in *different forms* – single words, longer explanations, ticked boxes and so on. Copy information when told to do so – and use your own words when that is necessary.

Unit 4 *What is being assessed?*

In this unit you will:

- find out about the skills on which you will be tested
- focus on each skill, moving from the simpler ones to those which are more difficult
- practise answering questions, and demonstrating your understanding.

Focus 1: Describe, select or retrieve information, events or ideas from texts and use quotation and reference to text.

In many ways, this is the easiest skill. You have to:
- find appropriate information
- write it down
- or put it into your own words.

Read this description, taken from a Humanities textbook, then work through the questions which follow.

The end of a city

San Francisco is close to the San Andreas Fault, where sections of the Earth's surface meet. Sometimes, they shift. Earthquakes result.

On 18 April 1906, at 5.13am, such a movement occurred. The 500 000 people who lived in San Francisco at that time were terrified. The first shock lasted 40 seconds, during which time much of the city collapsed.

The eyewitness reports give some sense of the drama. Enrico Caruso, a famous Italian opera singer, was staying at the Palace Hotel: "Everything in the room was going round. The chandelier was trying to touch the ceiling and the chairs were all chasing each other. Crash! Crash! It was terrible. Everywhere the walls were falling and clouds of dust were rising. My God! I thought it would never stop."

Streets moved up and down. Windows shattered. Church bells rang maniacally in church towers. People ran from their houses and rooms into the streets, screaming, in their night-clothes. Some carried valuables: photographs, bags, even pets; others cowered, holding their heads and howling; others ran, pointlessly and without direction; some were too stunned to even speak.

There was a ten second pause. Then another huge shock followed.

When it all stopped, the dust still had to settle. Looking around, the citizens of a once great city were devastated. Whole districts had fallen, or, apparently, sunk into the ground. In the downtown area, almost every building was destroyed.

Crying was everywhere, from those who were unscathed and from those poor souls who were buried. Hundreds died.

Five hours later, the second instalment of the tragedy began. A woman lit a fire in her apparently undamaged house, but her chimney had been affected and the roof of the kitchen set alight. The mains water pipes had burst in the quake, so there was no way of controlling the blaze. San Francisco burned – for three days and two nights.

Then, the rain fell. When the air cleared, only smouldering ruins remained. Old San Francisco was no more.

Task 1

Answer the questions below, and use the advice offered.

Question 1

Copy and complete this table, putting the events of the story into order.

What exactly happened at 5.13am?

Say when the first shock ended

Time	Event
5.13am	
	Shock finished
Three days and two nights later	

Find the phrase 'three days and two nights later', and write down what happened at that point.

Finally, find the event which was most important, in terms of the disaster, and happened between:
- *the end of the earthquake*
- *and the end of this story.*

Write down when it happened, and what it was.

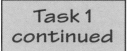

Task 1 continued

Question 2

List six things that happened while the Earth shook.

Relevance: = *Make sure they happened during the earthquake!*

Technique: = *Don't just copy out sections of the text – use a numbered list or bullet points.*

Advice: = *Find **six details** if you want **full mark**s.*

Question 3

Write down a sentence or phrase from the text which brings humour into the story.

Obviously, people laugh at different things, so this could be a difficult question. Don't select something which makes you laugh just because it is horrible. Perhaps there is something that is amusing because of the way it is said.

Question 4

Explain, in your own words, why San Francisco was destroyed. Refer to *both* major incidents.

*Take care with this question. Notice you have to find **two parts** to the disaster and explain what happened in each case.*

Question 5

Which word suggests that the world had gone mad?
a. shattered
b. maniacally
c. cowered

Since you are not allowed to use a dictionary in the examination, you need to:
- *find the words in the text (scan with your eyes or move your finger quickly over the text)*
- *read that section of the extract*
- *decide which is the most likely answer.*
It could be that you know exactly what the words mean – that will certainly help! However, read them 'in context': see how they are being used in this case.

Further Work

Once you have written your answers to the questions, share them with a friend, and agree the best responses between you.

Focus 2: Deduce, infer or interpret information, events or ideas from the text.

Deduce   =   work out from information provided
Infer   =   work out what is being said less obviously
Interpret =   put what you have deduced or inferred into your
              own words.

In this play, *Leaving on Friday* by Fran Landahl, a family is packing to move house.

James: My room's clear. Well, it's in boxes.

John: You're ready to go, then?

James: Sure am.

John: And happy too, it seems. Nothing affects you, does it? Record player safe?
            James nods. Right. Get it all downstairs, then. Just for once, try not to break anything
            on the way. Enough damage has been done already.
            James leaves. Kate enters.

Kate: We're getting closer. I don't know where to start in the kitchen, though.

John: Will we need it all?

Kate: I'm taking everything we can. I don't think the lino's worth moving, though. It'll break
            if we try to get it up.

John: Well, don't leave that fridge. We had to get one and be in with the latest fashion, didn't
            we? Then this happens.

Kate: Don't start again: everyone's got a fridge nowadays.

John: Yes. But we could use that money now…

Task 2

details

Question 1

**Choose two details from this extract which suggest when the play is set.
Explain your choices.**

*No precise dates are given: consider whether the play is set in the present day,
or some years ago (for example, discuss word choices, things that are not in
fashion anymore and so on).*

Question 2

**What, do you imagine, is the relationship between these characters?
Use details from the script to prove your points.**

*You can't skim through for this – read carefully, and examine how the characters
speak to each other – decide, for example, who is in control, who is most friendly
– and make logical decisions in the light of the evidence.*

This extract comes later:

> **John**: … And if it hadn't happened, there'd have been no need for all this.
>
> **Kate**: Not again. Let's just get on and get finished.
>
> **John**: The usual line: ignore it and it'll all be forgotten. Just like in Norfolk – that was when the village shop complained, wasn't it? Or was that when we were in Wales? I sometimes forget. So many incidents, I confuse them.
>
> **Kate**: John, please … James'll be back and he'll hear you …
>
> **John**: Oh, heaven forbid he should be reminded of what he's done. It was him that did it, wasn't it? The way you talk, I sometimes think it was me …

Question 3

Why is John angry with James?

The information is not made clear at this point. However, you can:
- *interpret John's suggestions about the past*
- *comment on the inference about whatever he has done most recently.*

Question 4

Using this extract, what can we deduce about the relationship between John and Kate?

Think about:
- *what they say*
- *how they say it*
- *how you can interpret this – rephrase and explain in your own words.*

Question 5

In the line which follows this extract, Kate says:
'That could never be. You always remind us that you're perfect.'

What is she implying about John?

Structure and organisation of texts =	the order of ideas, why one paragraph comes before another, looked at over the whole text
Grammatical features =	the precise choice of words and sentences and so on
Presentational features =	the visual shape and layout of texts.

Focus 3: **Comment on the structure and organisation of texts, including grammatical and presentational features at text level.**

Now, you must look at whole texts and see how they are put together.

This is part of a leaflet from a science museum. It celebrates the life and work of Sir Isaac Newton.

Sir Isaac Newton
1642–1727

Nowadays, we say, 'The penny dropped!' Isaac Newton was different. He was one very smart guy. In his case, the apple dropped, and he understood the concept of gravity. Very sharp!

Isaac Newton was born on Christmas Day, 1642, in Grantham in Lincolnshire, a few weeks after the death of his father. He was premature and feeble and was not expected to live until the next day. In fact, incredibly, he lived much longer than most people of those days, surviving for 84 years! And became one of the world's greatest scientists.

He did not just explain the idea of gravity. Amongst the significant achievements in his amazing life, he also:
- managed to split up light
- invented a whole new system of maths
- worked out the laws of motion.

And even found time to be an MP! Phew!

Even at school, he was unusual. Whilst other boys studied their Bibles on Sunday, as they were expected to do, he built model windmills, waterclocks and other mechanical devices. He made kites, too, and flew them at night, with fireworks attached to them. There was nothing usual about young Isaac Newton. He was 'cool'.

Unlike most people of his age, Newton did not believe in God; but he was another Christmas baby who did much to change the world. He was never conventional. His aim? To understand better how the natural world works.

Answer the questions below.

Question 1

The headings on the right summarise the information in the text boxes about Isaac Newton. Copy and draw lines to show which ones go together, or link them by letter/number. The first one has been done for you.

Text boxes

Headings

a) Isaac Newton was born on ...

(1) Things fell into place

b) Even at school, he was ...

(2) Lasting achievement

c) He did not just explain the ...

(3) Years of success!

d) Unlike most people of his ...

(4) The boy was different

e) Nowadays we say, 'The ...

(5) Achievements

Question 2

If this illustration had not been used, which other might have been included and why?

Make sure that your idea links directly with what is said in the leaflet, and explain clearly why you have chosen it.

Question 3

How is the idea that Sir Isaac Newton was *different* indicated in each of the text boxes? Find the specific words, or phrases – or type of language – used to stress this idea.

Resist the temptation to simply copy out everything each text box says. As requested, look for particular language. For example, you might wish to include 'incredibly' in your answer.

Question 4

Why does the leaflet use text boxes and the illustration, instead of just continuous writing?

In your answer, mention:
- *the likely audience*
- *the immediate effect on a reader*
- *the 'readability' of the details.*

Question 5

How is the idea of Christmas used at the end of the extract?

Reread the leaflet carefully; do not refer only to the final text box.

Further Work

The leaflet includes four 'sentences' which are not in formally correct English:
'Very sharp!'
'And became one of the world's greatest scientists.'
'And even found time to be an MP!'
'His aim?'

Write down why you think the writer does this.

This question is difficult! To answer it:
- *reread the relevant sections of the leaflet*
- *consider whether the effect would have been different if they had read:*
  'He was very clever.'
  'Also, he became …'
  'In addition, he found time …'
  and
  'What, we ask, was his aim?'
- *ask yourself who the target audience is, and why the chosen examples might be appropriate.*

Focus 4: Comment on the writer's use of language, including grammatical and literary features at word and sentence level.

Q: **How is this different from the skills just covered?**

A: Here, you will concentrate on the effect of language – and **very specific words** and **phrases** – within the text, rather than the text as a whole.

This extract comes from *The Heathen* by Jack London, a story set over 100 years ago. It reflects the time in which it was written, especially in its depiction of the relationship between Charley, the narrator and Otoo, from the island of Borabora. They survived a hurricane together, and have lived as brothers for 17 years, even exchanging names to bind themselves together. Frustratingly, though, Otoo continues to call Charley 'master'. At this point in the story, Charley's canoe has sunk and he is swimming to a ship, a schooner, which is throwing out lines to him. Unfortunately, a shark is circling:

By this time I was played out, and gave up hope. I was watching him manoeuvre for another attempt, when I saw a brown body pass between us. It was Otoo.

'Swim for the schooner, master!' he said. And he spoke gaily, as though the affair was a mere lark. 'I know sharks. The shark is my brother.'

I obeyed, swimming slowly on, while Otoo swam about me, keeping always between me and the shark, foiling his rushes and encouraging me.

By the time the schooner was thirty feet away I was about done for. I could scarcely move. The shark, finding that it was receiving no hurt, had become bolder. Several times it had nearly got me, but each time Otoo was there just the moment before it was too late. Of course Otoo could have saved himself any time. But he stuck by me.

'Good-by, Charley! I'm finished!' I just managed to gasp.

But Otoo laughed in my face, saying:

'I will show you a new trick. I will make that shark feel sick!'

He dropped in behind me, where the shark was preparing to come at me.

'A little more to the left!' he next called out. 'There is a line there on the water. To the left, master – to the left!'

I changed my course and struck out blindly. I was by that time barely conscious. As my hand closed on the line I heard an exclamation from on board. I turned and looked. There was no sign of Otoo. The next instant he broke surface. Both hands were off at the wrist, the stumps spouting blood.

'Otoo!' he called softly. And I could see in his gaze the love that thrilled in his voice.

Then, and then only, at the very last of all our years, he called me by that name.

'Good-by, Otoo!' he called.

Then he was dragged under, and I was hauled aboard, where I fainted in the captain's arms.

And so passed Otoo, who saved me and made me a man, and who saved me in the end.

Jack London

Task 4

Copy and complete the answers to the questions below. Where a choice of possibilities has been offered, choose the one you feel to be most appropriate.

Question 1

Otoo says: 'The shark is my brother.'
What is the effect of this sentence?

> *When he uses the metaphor/simile, Otoo is suggesting that ...*

Question 2

'Of course, Otoo could have saved himself any time. But he stuck by me.'
Why has the sentence been broken into two?

> *Because the sentence has been split, there is more emphasis/softness on the second part. The 'But ...' sounds very abrupt/strong and makes Otoo's act seem even more ...*

Question 3

The narrator says: 'I struck out blindly.' How is the meaning of this sentence made clear in the passage?

> *The exact meaning of the sentence is clear when we go on to read ...*
>
> *Obviously, the narrator was in a bad way, and because he was ...*

Question 4

The verb 'thrilled' is used to describe the emotion in Otoo's voice:
- **what impression of him does it give?**
- **write down another word, phrase or sentence which presents Otoo in the same light – and explain your choice.**

> *Otoo's voice sounds 'thrilled'. This makes the reader feel that Otoo is a man who ...*
>
> *'I will make that shark feel sick'/'gaily'/'as though the affair was a mere lark'/'laughed in my face'*
>
> *I think this choice is appropriate because ...*

Focus 5: Identify and comment on the writers' purposes and viewpoints, and the effect of the text on the reader.

Finally, we examine what a writer is trying to suggest or say and how his or her aim is achieved.

Read this article from a regional newspaper.

Having a whale of a time ...

According to the Japanese, when they kill whales 40% die instantly. A grenade harpoon explodes in the base of the neck, killing the whale with a shock to the brain. The average time to death is 2 minutes 30 seconds. That, say the Japanese, does not amount to cruelty.

Although whaling was banned in 1986, Norway continues to hunt whales in its own waters, and Japan kills them for 'scientific' reasons. That probably explains why it is still possible to buy whale meat in the country and why there are whale restaurants, with delicacies on the menu like whale heart and stewed whale tongue.

Now, however, the Japanese are fighting to have the international ban on whaling lifted. They do not just claim that whales can be slaughtered efficiently. They say that parts of the whale population are no longer under threat and that several species of the creature can be killed without causing any problems; their numbers have increased and there is no reason why they should not be hunted.

And scientists accept that though the Sperm Whale, Fin Whale, Blue Whale and Humpback Whale are still endangered, other species have recovered in recent times.

According to one expert in Tokyo's Tsukiji market, the problem for the West comes from how we perceive whales to be graceful and loving and majestic. "It's a cultural thing," he says. "You eat cows and sheep – no problem. But we like to eat whale meat. Why is that so different or so bad?"

According to Greenpeace, an organisation trying to protect the whales, the comparison is not so simple. Whales are not farmed, and they believe that if the ban is lifted, the whale population will be in trouble again. Certainly, when whaling was uncontrolled, it had disastrous results. Factory ships were introduced in 1870, with devastating consequences, so that, for example, 300 000 Blue Whales were butchered in the 1930s alone.

Campaigners say their fight has nothing to do with sensibilities. They are simply trying to save from extinction one of the most peaceful and beautiful creatures on the planet.

Question 1

How does the writer view the Japanese attitude to whaling?
In your answer, focus on the following quotations:
- 'According to the Japanese ...'
- 'That, say the Japanese, does not amount to cruelty ...'
- 'Japan kills for "scientific" reasons ...'

Try to explain what the writer is implying or suggesting: what can be inferred from the words?

Question 2

In the first three paragraphs, how does the writer reveal his own attitude to the killing and eating of whales?
In your answer, write about the vocabulary used.

You must, for instance, mention 'explodes in the base of the neck' and the likely effect of such a phrase on the reader.

Question 3

A Japanese expert explains a different point of view.
- Why does the writer include that opinion?
- What does he write to counter it?

Read what the Japanese man says, and then decide why it is used; and what follows in the next two paragraphs, and its effect.

Question 4

A recent survey revealed that 64% of Japanese people have never tasted whale meat.
Why does the writer leave this detail out?
In your answer, discuss:
- the weighting given to different opinions in the article
- the intended effect of the article.

Consider which opinion seems strongest and why; how the article begins and ends and the writer's viewpoint.

Unit Summary

Always give exactly the information required by the question.
Be prepared to respond to the:
- structure
- language
- implications
- writers' intentions.

All of these are to be addressed at word, sentence and whole text levels.

Unit 5 *How to read and respond to the test*

In this unit you will:

- focus on priorities in the test
- practise dealing with the test requirements.

Q: I understand the sort of questions I'm likely to be asked. But what, exactly, should I do in the test?

A: There are three distinct stages:

Stage 1

Use the reading time wisely. In the fifteen minutes available, attempt to read the three different text types (genres) on the paper. They will be connected by a theme.

Examiner's Tip: If you do not think you will have time, skim read the shortest text or the one with the greatest number of images.

Stage 2

When the test begins, concentrate on one text at a time:
- read through the questions first, before writing
- then deal with one question at a time, locating the required information.

Stage 3

Make sure, in every case, that you are answering exactly what the question demands. For example, look out for key words telling you whether you need to:
- list
- copy
- explain

Also, pay attention to the:
- number of marks available
- amount of space provided in your answer book.

If, for example, you have to locate certain information and there are three marks, you can usually assume you have to find three pieces of information.

Examiner's Tip: If you are asked to give details of how a theme or idea is developed and the answer booklet offers you a full page on which to write, produce a lengthy response!

Now read this review.

Cool C: As hot as it gets

Last Saturday I was at the Keyhole in London to see Cool C perform the first of his UK dates. I feared the worst. He could not be that hot and that cool. No one could.

When the main man came on stage, though, it was the real thing. He was so in your face, you could almost smell the burgers on his breath. His music was raw. Amazingly, too, it was better than on disk. Somewhere in the rhythms, there are touches of Eminem; and in the backing, you can sense Toploader lurking. Yet Cool C is his own man. His debut album, *Stanz*, due out next month, will be enormous.

He rocketed through a vibrant set, including his best-known singles: *Rip Me* – with purple mist rising all across the stage; *Santanda Da* – almost in the audience, touching hands, screaming; and *Take Me to the Chair* – on a huge silver scaffold, playing with a noose, sparks flying: ice cool in the mayhem.

After thirty minutes, he spun one final idea to the girls round the stage:

"You take me as you find me/ Gooseberry and gone/ Sour and remembered/ Till next summer, Sugarbabe."

Then there was instant dark, an explosion and no encore. The place was boiling, but no one as cool as Cool C comes back out.

Catch him on tour. I was wrong. He's even hotter than they say. And, very, very cool.

Task 1	For each of the questions on page 38, decide exactly what you are required to do: you are NOT answering the questions yet. Use this process.

Select the most important words: 'describe', 'find and copy', 'complete the table' or whatever.
Find how many details you should include.
Decide how much you are likely to have to **write**:

- see how many marks are available and consider the nature of the question
- consider what sort of response you are likely to have to produce in each case – for example, if you have to 'explain' something, your answer will be longer and more detailed than if you have to write down just one fact.

In this instance, you do not have a set amount of space given, so work out for yourself what is likely to be expected.

Task 1 continued

Now, go through the process with these questions. Don't answer them yet.

1. Write down one thing that Cool C does on stage.

   (1 mark)

2. Explain what the writer means when he says: 'you could almost smell the burgers on his breath'.

   (1 mark)

3. How does the writer structure his review?
   In your answer, discuss the:
   ● opening
   ● details of the performance
   ● effectiveness of the ending.

   (3 marks)

4. In the penultimate paragraph, which begins 'After thirty minutes …',
   explain how:
   ● the colon
   ● the forward slashes (/)
   are used by the writer.

   (2 marks)

5. What techniques are used to try to capture the excitement of the performance in the paragraph which begins: 'He rocketed through a vibrant set …'
   Consider the:
   ● language used
   ● punctuation.

   (4 marks)

Task 2

Now you can write your answers to the questions.

At the end of the Reading test, you will have to answer questions about all three texts with which you have been dealing.

Task 3

Read the three short extracts which follow, then answer the practice question.

From a school booklet:

Examination Instructions

1. Arrive for all exams on time.
2. Bring all necessary equipment.
3. Leave all books and bags in the locker area.
4. Remain silent when in the exam hall.
5. Go immediately to your seat.

From an autobiography:

> I well remember my first set of high school exams. I was so nervous, I dropped my pencil case as I entered the room, and everything clattered on the floor. Mrs Lindscombe went berserk. I scrabbled round to pick everything up, but people started laughing and we were all dispatched back to the corridor to sort ourselves out and "try again, properly this time…".

From a news broadcast:

> Further details are now known about the allegations into suspected malpractice during GCSE exams at a school in Surrey. The exam board sent inspectors to Candiside Grange School, following rumours that pupils were allowed to use notes during their History papers.

Question

The texts have different purposes and styles. Copy the text boxes below, then draw two lines from each text box in the middle column below. One line should link the text to its purpose. The other should link the text to the most appropriate style.

Purpose	**Text**	**Style**
entertain	school booklet	narrative
instruct	autobiography	informative
clarify	news broadcast	functional

Further Work

Think of two other types of text that could be on the same theme, and complete boxes for them, in the same way as has been done above.

Unit Summary

- ◆ Read carefully both the text and the question.
- ◆ Do exactly what the question asks and answer at an appropriate length.
- ◆ Concentrate on what you are doing: the wrong answer will gain no marks!

Unit 6 Prepare, write, check

In this unit you will:

- learn how to deal with preparation for the writing tasks
- practise using planning sheets
- employ a detailed writing process.

In the Writing test, you will be required to produce **two** pieces of writing.
One of these will require you to **write to persuade, argue or advise**.
The **other** question will ask you to **write to inform, explain or describe**.

The Writing test lasts for 1 hour 15 minutes.
There will be a
major task – 40 minutes
and a
minor task – 25 minutes.
You should also
check your work – 10 minutes.

Planning

For both tasks, your first priorities are to:
- recognise exactly what the task requires
- plan effectively for your response.

Begin by reading carefully through the question. Underline any important words, to help you stay 'on task' and help clarify what you must write about.

For example:

does not have to be a complete document

must give advice

could deal with local issues or problems

Write a <u>section</u> of an <u>advice sheet</u>, to be handed out in your <u>local area</u>, which focuses on how <u>people</u> should <u>look after their pets</u>.
You can choose to deal with <u>any pet or pets</u> you wish – for example, dogs, cats, hamsters or any others of *your choice*.

general audience

core task

select pets with which to deal

The details of tasks can be quite lengthy, so you need to read them carefully before you begin to write anything. Consider the following example.

1. *Exemplar question*

This is the opening from a short story by Isaac Asimov entitled *The Fun They Had*:

> Margie even wrote about it that night in her diary. On the page headed 17 May, 2155, she wrote, 'Today Tommy found a real book!'
>
> It was a very old book. Margie's grandfather once said that when he was a little boy *his* grandfather told him that there was a time when all stories were printed on paper.
>
> They turned the pages, which were yellow and crinkly, and it was awfully funny to read words that stood still instead of moving the way they were supposed to – on a screen, you know. And then, when they turned back to the page before, it had the same words on it that it had had when they read it the first time.

Imagine you are living in 2155, and looking back to the start of the twenty-first century. Write an essay to inform young people in 2155 about 'real books'.

Explain:
- **how important books used to be, and why**
- **how books were used**
- **about libraries, and why they were so valuable.**

Describe:
- **the sorts of books which were available**
- **the kinds of people who read them.**

| Task 1 | With a friend, select the words in the title that you would underline, to guide and inform the remainder of your work on this subject. |

2. Planning

In the test, you will get a planning sheet as part of your answer booklet. It will be divided into sections and will indicate how you might structure your writing.

For example:

Before you begin, jot down the ideas you will need to include:

How important were books?

Why?

Don't write in sentences! These boxes are for ideas only.

How books were used

Here, for example, you could jot down ideas about all the uses of books in school, for leisure, as found in libraries, and so on – and how often they were used.

The importance of libraries

Think about all the reasons why libraries are considered so important – there are even mobile libraries in country areas.

The sorts of books available

Consider the variety of books and forms of texts in libraries.

The sorts of people who read books

Widen your horizons here so that you are not just thinking about children: consider the old, researchers, even people on holiday and what they like to read.

Task 2

1. Now sketch out the boxes, and complete them, to produce a plan of your ideas.
2. When the boxes are complete, number the ideas you have written down in *each box*, so that you know what order to use them in your full written response.

For example:

> **How important were books?**
> Used for information (research) **4**   in schools **2**   law **6**
> religious books **8**   history **7**   universities **3**   maps **9**   medicine **5**
> knowledge and entertainment **1**
>
> **Why?**
> Passing information **3**   Only way to record things for centuries **1**
> Storehouse of ideas **2**   Used for teaching and learning **4**

3. Writing

Task 3

1. Decide whether you need an introduction and/or conclusion.
2. Write the response, using the notes you have made – there is no point in planning, then ignoring the ideas you have collected!

In the test
your writing will be assessed on your ability to:
- write effectively for a particular audience
- paragraph and/or organise your writing
- vary your sentence structures and punctuate well
- write accurately.

Task 4

check!

1. Check through your response with the above list in mind.
   Make sure:
- you have written for 'young people'
- you have paragraphed and organised your ideas so the response is easy to follow and flows smoothly
- your sentences are varied, interesting and correctly punctuated (remember that 'punctuation' means more than just capital letters and full stops!)
- your spelling is correct – check with a dictionary when you are just practising.
2. Correct what you can.

> *Unit Summary*
>
> In the test, make sure you:
> ◆ read the question carefully – 'take it to pieces' first
> ◆ plan in detail – sequence and prioritise your ideas
> ◆ follow your plan when writing
> ◆ check your work thoroughly.

Unit 7 Writing to persuade, argue, advise

In this unit, you will focus on writing to persuade, argue and advise by:
- practising with test-style questions
- using the techniques which will improve your marks.

Writing to argue

Q: What does 'writing to argue' mean? I know how to argue!

A: When writing to argue, we often:
- present a *situation* or *problem*
- write about it from a *particular viewpoint* (sometimes, but not always, our own)
- argue *for* that viewpoint, either:
  - by presenting *the opposite viewpoint, then arguing against it*

  or
  - by *arguing one case strongly*, whilst *all the time bearing in mind the other point* of view
- conclude by *summarising* the argument.

For example:

COULD SCHOOL MEALS BE BETTER? ← *Headline*

First paragraph explains the current situation

Let's face it, most of us have pretty grim memories of our school lunches. Those like myself, who are long in the tooth, remember times when there was no choice, and we were faced with bland awfulness: meat that was mostly yellow fat; lumpy potatoes, and over-cooked cabbage. But are things so much better today?

Body of text 'supports' school meals, then argues for improvement

Since the removal of the requirement that school meals should be nutritious and balanced, cafeteria systems across the country have gone straight for 'chips with everything'. Most students, it seems, have pizza and chips most lunchtimes. If there are any salads provided, they are usually grabbed by the teachers; and often there is not even water, just fizzy drinks.

They are educated in school about the need to eat fruit and vegetables, then fed grease, stodge and chemicals!

The only excuse, of any kind, could be that the young are at least eating what they want and choose. Yet they do not enjoy what they throw down their throats – they simply fill their stomachs; they are just responding, automatically, to peer pressure and a lack of real choice. Worse still, their diet is building problems for them in the future.

It is about time the government accepted the scale of the problem and acted. Legislation is needed, to make schools healthy eating environments. It is no good hoping that head teachers and governors will eventually improve the situation. Our children need rescuing from themselves, pizzas and chips: and today, not tomorrow.

Final paragraph points out that students' health and happiness is at risk from school canteens

---

Practice Question

(Do not answer this, just read it through):

Write a letter to your headteacher to **argue** that your school should move to a four-day working week.

Your address

The date

Head's name

School address

Dear ....,

situation or problem →

I am sure you are well aware of how hard the students work in this school. Like the teachers, we all want to see examination results improve. I am writing to you, therefore, with a suggestion which, I believe, could benefit the school enormously:

I suggest we move to a four-day working week.

the opposite viewpoint →

Such an idea is revolutionary. It will, no doubt, shock the school governors. They will say that we need as much time as possible in school, in order to learn; that in four days we could not get through the curriculum; and that if we were not in school, we would simply waste our time.

discourse markers →

However ... (Paragraph 3)

What is more ... (Paragraph 4)

It seems clear, therefore, that ... (Paragraph 5: Conclusion)

summary →

I hope that I have managed to convince you, and that the school week will change in the very near future.

Yours sincerely,

....

Task 1

Plan:
● two paragraphs (3 and 4), containing ideas in favour of the scheme
● a concluding paragraph, to sum up your argument.

Task 2 Complete the letter, using the discourse markers provided and the ideas in your plan.

Writing to persuade

Persuade

Q: What is the difference between persuading and arguing?

A: When you are persuading, you do not always have to consider so seriously 'the other side' of the case.

> For example, if you want to persuade your teacher to let you off homework, you are unlikely to spend time telling her why regular homework is a good thing!
>
> However, whether you are arguing a case, or persuading someone ...
> just state your case, or set out to counter a viewpoint ...
> many of your techniques will be the same.

For example:

1. **Rhetorical questions** – which do not require a direct answer, because it is clear the speaker already knows the answer. These are designed to create a particular effect:

question	suggests...
Should we leave the poor to starve in Africa?	We *must* help them.
Could anyone invent a sport more boring than golf?	It would be impossible.

2. **Emotive language** – which touches the reader's emotions: this often depends on creating strong images, or using powerful verbs, for example:

Just imagine the *tears of the orphaned children* ... .
Meanwhile, the family pets are *driven and dumped* in an *isolated part of town*, to *scavenge* for their own food if they can ... .

Task 3

Imagine you are going to persuade your friend to help you tidy the garden for an old person who lives nearby.

2 *examples*

Note down **two** examples of:
● rhetorical questions
and
● emotive language
you will use.

Practice Question

(Do not do the question, just read it, then complete the tasks below).

Write an article for your school magazine, to persuade the students to support Red Nose Day at your school.

Task 4

Plan the article, using the structure provided.

Requirement

Advice

1. Explain what the school intends to organise.

Say when and what will happen, and where; who is involved already and how much money might be raised.

2. Stress the benefits of Red Nose Day.

Mention where the money goes. Millions raised in past: £56 million in 2001.

3. Detail some activities students could do to help.

Suggest a range. Stress fun.

4. Explain what students should do if they wish to be involved.

Mention important contacts, getting a team together and so on.

5. Conclude by explaining how to have fun planning an event.

Give examples of the enjoyment you and your friends will have.

Task 5

Now write your actual answer to the question.

 Examiner's Tip: Remember to use rhetorical questions, and emotive language.

Writing to advise

Q: Isn't advice usually simple? All we have to say is: 'Don't do it …' or 'Think twice …'.

A: Often, advice is more detailed. It is not just a matter of giving someone your opinion; for the advice to have real value, it must seem sensible. To do this, you need to convince the reader – or listener – that you have covered 'every angle'.

So, you might wish to consider *all the available information*, then:
● give *a clear piece of advice*, saying exactly what should be done

or
● *offer alternatives*, because the situation is not simple.

Task 6

Work in pairs.
1. To practise offering advice in a relatively simple situation:
   Imagine a friend is really panicking about how to revise for school examinations.
   What advice would you offer?

   Consider:
   ● what to do some weeks before the exams
   ● how to organise last minute exam revision
   ● what to do on the day of an exam.

2. Now imagine a much more difficult situation:
   Imagine a friend is having lots of trouble at home and is threatening to run away.
   What advice would you offer?

   Consider:
   ● the nature of the problems
   ● alternative ways of coping
   ● your considered opinion.

Practice Question

Here, we are practising producing a response to a *minor task*. It means that you will write *less*, but must be as precise as possible in your use of language:

As 'A Friend', you write an advice column for a teenage magazine. Respond to these two letters.

Letter 1:

> Dear Friend,
> I really want to start doing a paper round after school, but my mum says I've got too much homework, and that's more important. What can I do?

Letter 2:

> Dear Friend,
> I'm 12 years old. My parents never let me stay out after nine o'clock at night. It's not fair, is it? How can I get round them?

Task 7

Plan your responses.

Letter 1:

- **Importance of homework**
- **Advantages of doing paper round**
- **How to respond to mother**

Letter 2:

- **Parents' concerns**
- **What time people of your age mostly come in and why**
- **Whether, therefore, parents are right or wrong**
- **What to say to them/how to negotiate with them**

Task 8

Now write your replies.

Further Work

Compare your replies with real replies from an Agony Aunt in a popular magazine. How professional sounding were yours, compared with the real ones?

Unit Summary

◆ Make sure you are doing exactly what the question requires: argue, persuade or advise as requested.
◆ Use key techniques you have learned (for example, rhetorical questions).
◆ In your planning, include detail.
◆ Write as accurately as you can.

Unit 8   *Writing to inform, explain, describe*

In this unit, you will focus on writing to inform, explain and describe by:

● reviewing what these forms of writing involve
● practising a number of key skills related to them.

Writing to inform

Q: Is this just a matter of providing information?

A: You will have to give information but, in the writing test, two key things to remember are:

● use sufficient detail
● write effectively – that is, achieving your purpose.

Remember that (unless you are told otherwise) you will be marked on:
● the range and organisation of your ideas
● variety and appropriateness of sentences and vocabulary
● punctuation and accuracy
in exactly the same way as for the other writing tasks.

Therefore, if the organisation of ideas is a key thing, you must focus on the main organisational device in English – your sentences.

| Task 1 | Imagine you have stopped a passer-by, to ask her how to reach the local leisure centre. She replies: |

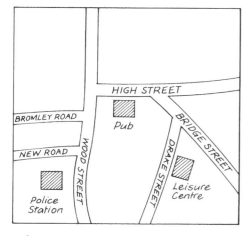

"Right, this is Wood Street. Straight down here. 100 metres. On your left, the police station. Steps at the front, you can't miss it. OK. Another two roads on your left. After them, first right. You'll see 'The Angel': big pub, on the right – there'll be music. Past it, then first right and right again. Then, straight on. It's easy. You can't miss it."

Write out the directions, and:
- put them into effective sentences
- vary your sentence structures, using:
  - long and short sentences (sometimes a simple instruction will work, such as 'Continue for 50 metres')
  - simple and complex sentences
  - commas, and other punctuation, as appropriate.

Practice Question	You are going on holiday for a fortnight. You must leave all necessary details to inform your neighbour how to look after your pet.

Task 2	Plan your answer.

In this task, write:
- factually
- precisely: do not confuse your neighbour.

Include:
- all that is necessary
- nothing that isn't!

> **Examiner's Tip.** The verb forms most likely to be used in informative writing are:
> - future ('*You will need to ...*')
> - imperative ('*Please turn off ...*').

Temporal connectives may be useful:
- then
- later
- on the second day

Use these headings to plan your response.

- **Type, name, temperament**

- **Important considerations: House alarm? Cat flap? Keeping animals apart? Where things are kept and so on.**

- **Feeding: regularity, amounts, diet, treats, what to avoid and so on.**

- **Exercise and/or general care, cleaning, details of vet and so on.**

- **Contact details in case of emergency.**

Task 3	Now write the full response, using your plan.

Writing to explain

Explain

Q: What is special about writing to explain?

A: This is a form of writing which you will use in many subject areas, for example writing up experiments, telling your teacher why the Romans invaded Britain and so on. However, problems sometimes stem from the fact that students assume the reader already knows about what they are explaining.

To avoid this:
- assume that the reader knows nothing: make everything very clear
- structure everything sensibly, so that there is logical progression in what you say.

For example, if you were explaining what the best features of a holiday destination were:

Prioritise information and give *relevant detail*	You wouldn't concentrate on how long it took to catch the train to the airport.
Sequence information *logically*	You would be unlikely to describe the flight home as your first point.
Use discourse markers, especially those concerned with *cause and effect*.	'The air-conditioning is poor in the hotel, *so* expect to have sleepless nights ...'.

Task 4

To see how difficult it is to explain some things clearly:

1. Write an explanation of how to tie:
   a tie
   or
   shoelaces.

2. Read the explanation to a friend, who must do exactly what you say.

3. Try again!

Practice Question

Write an item to be included in a 'welcome pack' to be given to pupils when they first arrive at your school.
Your task is to explain how a typical school day is organised.

Task 5

Produce a detailed plan.

You might want to mention:

- lesson times
- bells
- registrations
- the number of lessons
- lunchtime arrangements
- the use of fields and particular areas of the school like libraries.

Bear in mind your target audience.

Concentrate on clear chronological order, so that your account moves forward in time.

Once again, temporal connectives are likely to be useful:
- next
- afterwards
- following this
but use causal ones, too (such as 'As a result ...' and so on).

Avoid using 'I'. The explanation is what matters, not your feelings here.

Task 6

Write your item.

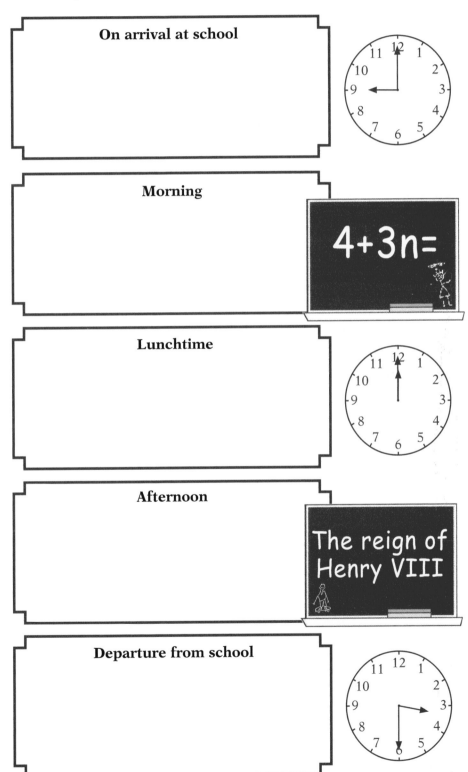

On arrival at school

Morning

4+3n=

Lunchtime

Afternoon

The reign of Henry VIII

Departure from school

Writing to describe

Describe

Q: We focus on description all the time in English, but what does it mean to me in the test situation?

A: The key here is probably to focus on two areas:

Close and *evocative* detail, and *precise* use of language.

FOCUS — Detail Language

This is true whether the descriptive writing is:

- a description of something or someone 'real'

or

- an imaginative description such as: 'Life in the year 3002'.

Be prepared to have to describe something from the past, present or future. Whatever you describe, your description is more likely to be believable if you focus on detail, rather than writing vaguely, using just general ideas.

Task 7	Here are two extracts. One is written impersonally, the other reads more like a story. Do they contain powerful images? Is there any word or phrase that could be more precise? Discuss with a friend whether one is better than the other.

Extract 1

The team bus came through the city centre, and a red tide of thousands surged forward towards the barriers, hoping to see the three gleaming trophies held aloft.

Extract 2

Amy looked down from the window on to the thousands lining the street below. In a few minutes, the team would pass by. She was so excited, it felt as if her heart had filled her ribcage and was throbbing like some demented monster.

Examiner's Tip:

An evocative detail is one that calls a picture to mind, so putting powerful images in your writing as well as feelings is vital.

Practice Question

Complete two pieces of writing:
1. Describe, in detail, your journey into your nearest town or shopping centre.
2. Imagine your local town or shopping centre has been totally renovated or modernised. Describe it.

Task 8

Plan both responses.

1. Being descriptive here gives you the opportunity to offer more than just the basic route. You might wish to include the smells from a local bakery, the sounds from the factory or from the farm, and so on.

- Directions
- Significant landmarks

- The buildings
- The atmosphere
- The shops
- Other features

2. You might wish to use imagery – or an imaginative approach, such as describing it as if you are actually there.

Task 9

Write your descriptions.

Further Work

Describe a journey into London shortly after the Great Fire of 1666.

Unit Summary

Ensure that when you write to inform, explain or describe:
- ◆ your ideas are clear and well organised
- ◆ you use a variety of appropriate sentence structures
- ◆ you include sufficient and appropriate detail
- ◆ where relevant you use evocative and powerful language.

Unit 9   *The spelling test*

In this unit, you will:

learn how the spelling test is conducted
practise by using a similar format.

In addition to the Reading test and the Writing test, there is also
a Spelling test.

This is separate from the main tests, and can be taken at any
time in the school year. The words on which you are tested
cover certain spelling patterns; some will be from a list of words
supplied by the government's education department, just as in
the practices which follow.

In the real Spelling test, you will have a text in front of you.
Certain words from it will be missing.

Your teacher will:

1. read the whole text, including the missing words (which are
    on his/her copy)
2. read it again, pausing after each word that is missing on
    your copy, so that you can put in the missing word.

Examiner's Tip: There is **no time limit** on the test – you don't have to fill
the words in within five minutes, so if you don't hear a word
properly, **ask your teacher to repeat it.**

You do not have to guess which actual words are missing – simply write down the word read
out by your teacher.

To practise this skill, you have what might prove a slightly easier task! You can do the task on
the facing page in two ways.

Either:

• Read it to a partner (without giving them the alternative spellings) and they write down the
   words, which you then check together

Or

• Work through it on your own, writing down your answers.

Read this autobiographical extract, and select the words which are spelt correctly.

First day at high school

I had received/recieved instructions from my sister: "Do'nt/Dont/Don't argue with the teechers/teachers. They use any opportunity/oppertunity to give you a detention. In the begining/beginning, they might give you a chance, but they cant/can't be trusted. Rember/Remember to be careful/carefull."

Basicly/Basically, I was terrified. My primery/primary school had been friendly, but I knew that in the high school there would be no where/nowhere to hide. And I hardly/hardley knew anythink/anything.

Where/Were would I find the toliets/toilets? Would the Year 11s steal you're/your sweets? Does everybody end up hating/hateing assembly? Would every body/everybody laugh if I started crying/crieing?

"I hope it goe's/goes well," said my mum.

I feared I might get a nasty surprise/suprise.

"You've got your dads'/dad's lucky pen. You'll be fine," said mum.

Wow! That would frighten the bullies!

Once you have finished, go through your choices and write a brief explanation (if you can) saying *why* you chose the spellings that you did.

Think about the key conventions you have covered, such as when to double consonants – or the difference in meanings between homophones.

Task 2

Now follow the same process for this extract, either testing a friend, or working through it on your own.

Select the correct spellings from this adventure story.

Meenwhile/Meanwile/Meanwhile, I ran straight/strate towards the beach. It had been beautifull/beautiful during the day, but at night it seemed to have aquired/acquired a sinister atmosphere.

Alot/A lot of the waves were pounding against the cliffs/cliffs' and comeing/coming closer to the boats which had been pulld/pulled clear of the tide. The noise on the pebbles stoped/stopped any chance of hearing if any one/anyone was following.

My chest was realy/really painful. I thought of the weird/wierd man who had warned me not to mess with gangster's/gangsters' friends. I should have lissened/listened. I rumaged/rummaged in my bag and pulled out the whistle. This might be my last opportunity/oppertunity, but should I blow it? Would Steven be anywhere around to hear?

I knew my strenght/strength would soon be gone. I didn't want to die without a murmer/murmur. Why shouldn't I go out noisly/noisily?

Whatever else, I'd soon know if they were their/there. I put the whistle to my lips and blew.

Further Work

Once you have made a note of why you chose the spellings you did, try composing your own spelling dictation or test for a friend. You may wish to include some of the same spellings but, if possible, choose new ones that you know can cause problems.

Consider:

- pluralisation: for example, 'es' endings, and words ending in 'y', 'f' and vowels

- similar word endings, such as 'cian', 'tion' and 'sion', and homophones

- prefixes and suffixes (for example, 'un', 'ir', 'ful' and so on)

- apostrophes.

Unit Summary

◆ The Spelling test is separate from the main two tests.
◆ You will only be required to fill in spaces in a text which your teacher will read to you.
◆ Revising some of the key conventions of spelling, and the exceptions, will help you to succeed; learning a list can help, but is better if linked to the conventions.

Answers

Task 1: received, don't, teachers, opportunity, beginning, can't, remember, careful, basically, primary, nowhere, hardly, anything, where, toilets, your, hating, everybody, crying, goes, surprise, dad's.

Task 2: meanwhile, straight, beautiful, acquired, a lot, cliffs, coming, pulled, stopped, anyone, really, weird, gangsters', listened, rummaged, opportunity, strength, murmur, noisily, there.

Unit 10 Success in the tests

In this unit, you will :
- review what each test consists of
- revise key ways of tackling the main two tests
- focus on using the available time most profitably.

The Reading test

Time: 15 minutes reading
        75 minutes to complete the test

Read the texts as thoroughly as you can during the 15 minutes allowed.

In the test itself:

Concentrate on one extract at a time.
- Read the first question.
- Locate the information.
- Answer the question.

Remember the levels of question difficulty:
- find information only
- find information and explain
- find information, and quotation and explain.

Remember:
- take note of the significant words, telling you precisely what to do
- notice how many marks are available and respond accordingly.

For example:
'Select three actions by Hildegarde and explain what they tell us about her.'
                                                                    (6 marks)

With 6 marks, you might assume there is:
- 1 mark for each action
- 1 mark for each explanation.

- expect to have to produce longer answers if:
  - there are more marks
  - you have been given more space on the page to respond.

Work through each question in the same way.

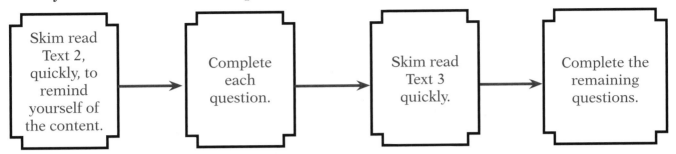

When you have answered all the questions on Text 1

| Skim read Text 2, quickly, to remind yourself of the content. | → | Complete each question. | → | Skim read Text 3 quickly. | → | Complete the remaining questions. |

Skim read by casting your eyes quickly over the text: pick up key words, or names, or the first lines of paragraphs, just to remind yourself of the basic content.
Do not reread the whole text, word by word.

When you have finished

- Check each answer carefully.
  Try to read your work as if you have never seen it before.
  That will help you to spot:
  – instances when you could have failed to answer fully the question which has been asked
  – any sections which do not make sense
  – any words which you have omitted
  – incorrect spellings which might confuse the marker.
- Make any necessary changes.

Remember:
It is better to improve something, even if it means making alterations.
However, make sure that your alterations are as neat as possible.

Whatever happens, it is vital that your work is legible: so do not scribble out mistakes and make it difficult for the marker.
Put a single line through any words or phrases that you wish to change:

~~Mayking it luke betr~~ which makes it look as neat as possible.

| Task 1 | If someone is about to take the Reading test, which are the five most important pieces of advice they should be offered?
List your ideas. |

pieces of advice

The Writing test

Time: 75 minutes
consisting of: a major task – 45 minutes
a minor task – 30 minutes

Writing skills being tested: the ability to write to:

argue   **persuade**   **advise**   **explain**   **inform**   **describe**

Major task	Spend about: 10 minutes reading and planning

Spend about: 10 minutes reading and planning
30 minutes writing
5 minutes checking.

1. Reading and planning

- Read the material.
- Identify exactly what the task involves.
  For example:
  'Write a <u>letter</u> to a <u>friend</u>, to offer <u>advice</u> on <u>where</u> to go for a <u>holiday next summer</u>.'
- Complete the planning process:
  – write down your ideas
  – number them, to indicate the logical order in which you will deal with them.

2. Writing

Produce your response as neatly and accurately as you can.

> **Remember:**
> There is no point in producing planned notes and then not following them in your actual response. Do not forget to include:
> - paragraphs
> - varied sentences
> - a range of appropriate punctuation
> - powerful or evocative vocabulary (where appropriate).

3. Checking

To make sure your response is as perfect as possible in test conditions, try to read it as slowly in your head as if you were reading it out loud.
This technique should help you spot errors in:
- general expression
- vocabulary – for instance, make sure that all your words are suitable for the intended audience
- punctuation
- spelling.

Correct your work as appropriate.

Minor task	Use the same techniques, although you will not be writing as much. Spend: 5 minutes reading and planning 20 minutes writing 5 minutes checking.

Task 2	If you had just 60 seconds to offer your class some advice on how to be successful in the Writing test, what would you say? Decide which advice is most important if they are to be successful.

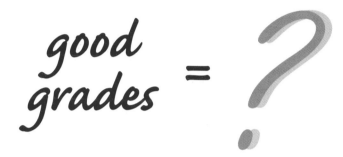

Unit Summary

If you know exactly what the tests involve and how to cope with them, you are much more likely to do yourself credit. After all, they are there for you to show what you have learned, not to catch you out.

Avoid the temptation to panic in test conditions:

◆ deal with each test in an organised way
◆ use the information and advice you have been given.

Final checklist

Check through this list to see that you have covered all the necessary skills and revision areas. The right-hand column tells you which Unit (or Units) you can refer back to, if you need to redo or relearn a skill.

Do you know ...?   **Go to Unit**

● When the tests take place	Check with your teacher now
● What each test involves	1, 6, 9, 10

Have you prepared for the Reading test by learning about ... ?

● The genres you could encounter	2
● The sorts of questions you will be asked	2, 3, 4
● How to deal with the questions	5 & 10
● How to check and improve your answers	10

Have you prepared for the Writing test by learning about ... ?

● Planning responses	6–8
● Writing to persuade	7
● Writing to argue	7
● Writing to advise	7
● Writing to inform	8
● Writing to explain	8
● Writing to describe	8
● How to check and improve your answers	10

Have you prepared for the Spelling test by ... ?

● Practising the type of task you will be given	9
● Revising key spelling patterns and conventions	9